The Olive Branch.

THE REPORT OF THE REV. SEPTIMUS TUSTIN, D. D.,

CLERICAL DELEGATE

FROM

THE GENERAL ASSEMBLY WHICH HELD ITS SESSIONS AT PEORIA, ILL.,

IN MAY, 1863,

TO

THE GENERAL ASSEMBLY WHICH HELD ITS SESSIONS AT PHILADELPHIA, PA.,

IN MAY, 1863,

ON THE OCCASION OF INAUGURATING A FRATERNAL CORRESPONDENCE BETWEEN THOSE BODIES, AFTER A CONSTRAINED INTERRUPTION OF FRIENDLY GREETINGS OF MORE THAN A QUARTER OF A CENTURY, PRESENTED TO THE GENERAL ASSEMBLY HOLDING ITS SESSIONS IN NEWARK, N. J.,

IN MAY, 1864.

WASHINGTON, D. C.:
McGILL & WITHEROW, PRINTERS AND STEREOTYPERS.
1864.

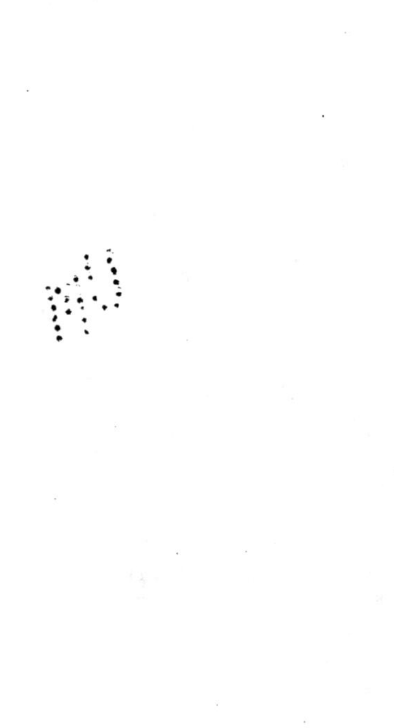

REPORT.

The year of our Lord 1837, was rendered memorable, throughout christendom, by the division of the Presbyterian Church in the United States of America. With respect to the *causes* which led to this great result, it is unnecessary if not improper, for your delegate to speak in this report. The learned and pious leaders of our sacramental host, considered disruption as necessary to secure the doctrinal purity of the Church. A large portion of the rank and file concurred in the eventful measure and for the same reason. Others acquiesced, and deemed a dismemberment preferable to a bitter and protracted theological war, the merits of which many of them did not comprehend. In many cases, however, the hearts of God's people, in both sections of the Church, continued to be linked together by indissoluble fetters which could not be disturbed even by the fearful shock which rent the Church in twain.

For more than a quarter of a century, *Time*, in his steady and irresistible flight, has been shedding down his salutary influences on the melancholy scenes of other years, the asperities of the painful crisis have subsided; the causes, real or supposed, of dissatisfaction have disappeared; and the hearts of the great Presbyterian family, like broken globules of quicksilver, have been gradually approaching nearer and nearer to each other, and indications are not wanting that ere long they will rush into one great heart of Christian love, cemented and adorned by a united ecclesiastical fellowship. So clear and decisive were the evidences of this blessed fact furnished to the General Assembly during its sessions at Columbus, Ohio, in 1862, that the Chairman of the Committee of Correspondence, the Rev. Septimus Tustin, D. D., felt constrained to gratify these pious demands of our people, from different sections of the country, by presenting, in behalf of said Committee, the following report which was unanimously and cordially adopted:

In the General Assembly of the Presbyterian Church in the United States of America, in session at Columbus, Ohio, the matter of a fraternal correspondence, by Commissioners, with the General Assembly of the Presbyterian Church (New School) in session at Cincinnati, Ohio, being duly considered, is decided as follows:

This Assembly having considered certain overtures sent to it by a few of the Presbyteries under its care, proposing that steps should be taken by it towards an organic union between this Church and the Church under the care of the Presbyterian General Assembly, New School; and having determined against the course proposed in said overtures, has also been informed that the other General Assembly has, about the same time, come to a similar conclusion on similar overtues laid before it by a certain number of its own Presbyteries. Of its own motion, this General Assembly, considering the time to have come for it to take the initative in securing a better understanding of the relations which it judges are proper to be maintained between the two General Assemblies, hereby proposes, that there shall be a stated annual and friendly interchange of Commissioners between the two General Assemblies, each body sending to the other one minister and one ruling elder, as Commissioners, year by year, the said Commissioners to enjoy such privileges in each body to which they are sent, as are common to all those now received by this body from other Christian denominations.

The Moderator of this Assembly will communicate this deliverance to the Moderator of the other Assembly, to be laid before it, with our Christian salutations.

The Committee of Foreign Correspondence, having been enlarged in view of the magnitude of this subject, consisted of the following persons, viz: Rev. Septimus Tustin, D. D., Chairman; Rev. Robert J. Breckenridge, D. D., LL. D., George W. Musgrave, D. D., LL. D., James Hoge, D. D.,

Rev. J. Y. Mitchell, Rev. A. J. Reynolds, Ruling Elders; Mr. S. E. Weir, and Mr. D. C. Rayburn.

In compliance with the suggestion in the close of the report the Rev. C. C. Beatty, D. D., Moderator, forwarded the foregoing document to the Rev. George Duffield, D. D., Moderator of the other Assembly in session at Cincinnati, accompanied with a judicious and fraternal letter, requesting him to bring this overture before that Assembly at the earliest practicable period.

Accordingly, when the Assembly convened in Philadelphia in May, 1863, among the first business taken up, (the Rev. Henry B. Smith, D. D., of New York City, having been chosen Moderator,) was the overture of the Assembly which met a year before in Columbus, Ohio. After some discussion, the paper was referred to the following Committee, viz: Rev. Samuel T. Spear, D. D., Rev. Samuel H. Cox, D. D., LL. D., Rev. Samuel H. Gridley, D. D., Mr. William H. Booth, and the Hon. Chancey N. Olds.

On the succeeding day, the following response was presented and unanimously adopted by a standing vote:

The Committee, to whom was referred the communication from the General Assembly of the Presbyterian Church in the United States of America, that met at Columbus, Ohio, in May, 1862, addressed to this General Assembly, and proposing a "stated, annual, and friendly interchange of Commissioners between the two General Assemblies," recommend the adoption of the following resolutions:

Resolved, 1. That this Assembly, with heartfelt pleasure and Christian salutations, accept the proposition thus made, hoping and praying that it may result "in securing a better understanding of the relations," which, in the judgment of this Assembly, "are proper to be maintained between the two Assemblies."

2. That, in accordance with the suggestion of the Moderator of the Assembly that met at Columbus, Ohio, in May, 1862, that this interchange of Commissioners should commence at the earliest practicable period, the Rev. Robert W. Patterson, D. D., and the Hon. William H. Brown, Principals, and the Rev. Arthur Swazey and Mr. Oliver H. Lee, Alternates, all of the Presbytery of Chicago, be appointed Commissioners to represent this General Assembly in the General Assembly now in session at Peoria, Ill.

3. That it be suggested that future General Assemblies of the two branches of the Presbyterian Church in the United States, hereafter, designate each other respectively by the places in which their sessions are appointed to be held.

4. That a certified copy of this action be at once transmitted to the Moderator of the General Assembly now in session at Peoria, Ill., and that the Commissioners appointed be requested to repair to that body, and express to them the fraternal and Christian regards of this General Assembly.

It was ordered that the substance of this report be communicated by telegraph to the General Assembly now in session at Peoria, Ill. Also that the Delegates from this Assembly be, in the same way, informed of their appointment.

On the 23d of May, the following telegram was transmitted by the Rev. Dr. Darling, and was received by the Rev. Dr. Morrison, Moderator of the Assembly then in session at Peoria, Illniois :

"PHILADELPHIA, *May* 22, 1863.

To the Moderator of the General Asssembly in session at Peoria:

The General Assembly of the Presbyterian Church now in session at Philadelphia, have unanimously appointed Delegates to represent them in your honorable body.

By order of the Assembly :

HENRY DARLING, *Clerk.*"

On the same day, 23d of May, the following proceedings were had in the Assembly at Peoria, viz :

The Committee of Correspondence reported by Rev. Dr. Blackwood, its chairman, the following nominations of delegates to represent this Assembly in the General Assembly of the Presbyterian Church now in session at Philadelphia, viz : the Rev. Septimus Tustin, D. D., Principal, and Rev. John Hall, D. D., alternate, and ruling elders, Hon. George Sharswood, principal, and Mr. John M. Harper, alternate. The Committee further suggested that the permanent clerk intimate to the Moderator of the Assembly in Philadelphia, the action of this body.

The committee consisted of the Rev. Wm. Blackwood, D. D., Rev. J. A. Morgan, and Rev. James Rowland, and James P. Tustin, and C. Byles, Ruling Elders.

The report was adopted, and on motion of the Rev. R. A. De Lancey it was ordered, that the permanent clerk be further directed to telegraph to the delegates just appointed by this Assembly, and inform them of their appointment.

In accordance with the foregoing proceedings, a telegram from Rev. William E. Schenck, D. D., permanent clerk, was received on the same day, by your clerical delegate in Philadelphia, and after consultation with all the delegates, principals, and alternates, was placed in the hands of the Rev. P. H. Fowler, D. D., who promptly and courteously communicated it to the Assembly ; whereupon it was ordered that the name of the Rev. Septimus Tustin, D. D., the only delegate present, be placed upon the roll.

It was made the order of the day, (25th of May, at 4½ o'clock, p. m.,) to hear the delegates from the General Assembly of the Presbyterian Church in session at Peoria.

At the appointed hour the Assembly was fully attended, and a large number of persons from other churches, attracted by the occasion, were in attendance.

Oppressed by the solemnity and importance of the high mission which had been, in part, confided to him, your delegate ventured, without instruction from his brethren, but with a proper sense of dependence upon God for direction to submit the following remarks :

Mr. Moderator and Brethren of the Assembly :

In the year of our Lord 1837 a violent ecclesiastical convulsion was felt in the heart of this city. By that convulsion the great Presbyterian Church was rent in twain, like the vail of the temple, from the top to the bottom. From that time down to the present, a period embracing a full quarter of a century, we have been two distinct peoples; bearing, it is true, the same name, and rejoicing in the same sublime symbol of faith, but still separate in our action and alienated in our affections.

With respect to the causes, real or imaginary, of that disruption, it would be inexpedient if not indecorous for me to speak at this time and in this presence. Some things, however, ought to be named, even though it should cover us with shame and self-condemnation. We have indulged in a bitterness of spirit toward each other not warranted by the Gospel we profess. We have exhibited prejudices for which we can find no justification. We have uttered words of unkindness and reproach which we can well afford to have obliterated, not only from our own recollection, but from the remembrance of God.

The question is frequently propounded by lips upon which have often trembled the words of prayer and supplication for the unity and prosperity of our Zion, "Shall we be always thus separated? Shall the barriers which now separate us never be removed? Shall we never become what we once were, a united, happy, prosperous Church, the praise and the glory of the whole land?"

In reply to these tender and anxious interrogatories, I have to say that, in my representative character, I am not authorized to express a judgment either favorable or adverse. I might, if it would answer any valuable purpose, speak of individual opinions and wishes, but not of the embodied sentiment of the Church court which I represent.

One thing, however, I am authorized to say—that so far as we are concerned the strife is at an end. The fierce war-cry that grated so long upon the heart of piety has died away into an echo so indistinct as to be scarcely distinguishable. Our ecclesiastical war-steeds, if I may so speak, are reclining amidst the olive groves of peace.

I come to you bearing aloft the trophies of fraternal love and affection—for love has its triumphs as well as hate; peace as well as war. I come to invite you back to our confidence and esteem. I come to express to you the wishes of my brethren, that the blessing of God, in its richest manifestations, may rest upon you individually and collectively; that harmony may characterize all your deliberations; that a heavenly influence may so pervade your hearts as that nothing shall occur to mar the beauty and symmetry of the body of Christ.

By the kindness and courtesy of my venerable and honored friend, the Moderator of the last General Assembly, which met a year ago at Columbus, Ohio, I was placed at the head of the "Committee of Foreign Correspondence." This position soon enabled me to ascertain the views and feelings of my brethren from different sections of the Church, on this interesting question. I found that while some difference of opinion prevailed with respect to the reunion of these two bodies at the present time, there was but one sentiment in reference to the propriety and desirableness of an interchange of Christian salutations through the medium of annually appointed delegates.

Having heard, whether rightfully or not I am not prepared to say, that you were discussing this same subject in your General Assembly at Cincinnati, Ohio, the committee of our Assembly hastened to anticipate your action, and thus secure the honor of inaugurating a measure so creditable to the source where it might first originate. It may have been ungenerous, but candor obliges me to confess that the committee was ambitious of that high distinction. You, Mr. Moderator and the Brethren of this Assembly, will, I am sure, in such a case, pardon our aspirations. Accordingly the committee reported in favor of immediate action by the Assembly, and actually nominated a worthy brother, (Rev. Robert Davidson, D. D.,) who should be the bearer of our Christian and friendly salutations, with the pleasing expectation that you would reciprocate our well-meant courtesies.

Some of the brethren, however, thought this action too hasty and precipitate for so grave a subject, and proposed a more sedate and deliberate proceedure. With a view of securing unanimity on a measure so dear to many hearts, the committee surrendered their original report, and presented the paper which has been read in your hearing as a substitute. This paper was not only unanimously, but I feel warranted in saying cordially, adopted by the Assembly.

Having learned through the telegraph, of your favorable action on the subject, the Assembly now in session at Peoria, Illinois, have, through the same medium, authorized me to represent them in part in this Assembly.

I accept this appointment with unfeigned satisfaction. I am sincerely grateful to my brethren for the distinguished honor which they have thus bestowed upon me. I regard it as the crowning glory of my life. In my declining years and enfeebled health, (pardon this personal allusion,) it comes like the breath of the vernal morning to the fevered and aching brow.

While I would thus express my high appreciation of the privilege extended to me by my brethren of representing them in this Assembly, I am also grateful to you, Mr. Moderator and Brethren of this Assembly, for your prompt and courteous attention to their communications on a subject of vital interest to our common Zion. I can only repay you by my earnest prayers that divine and celestial influences may descend so plenteously upon you as that love shall beam from every eye, distil from every lip, shower from the fingers of every hand, and create around this Assembly an atmosphere which angels will descend to inhale, and in which God himself will delight to dwell.

I cannot close these brief remarks without adding a word in relation to a subject not remotely akin to that which is now claiming our attention. The last quarter of a century has been signalized by the spirit of division which has pervaded all the departments of Church and State. Churches have divided—presbyteries have divided—synods have divided—General Assemblies have divided—conferences have divided—conventions have divided—and last, though not least, our beloved country, in some sense, has divided. Different portions of our once happy people are now arrayed in hostile attitude, and are pouring out each other's blood like water upon the ground. The wail of sorrow and anguish is heard from ten thousand homes and hearts throughout the land—"Rachel weeping for her children, and refusing to be comforted, because they are not."

The question is pertinent, whether the disintegrating spirit which has been fostered in our Churches has not had some considerable influence in producing this last great disruption, over which we all lament and mourn. I strongly incline to the judgment expressed on this subject by your venerable Moderator, in his admirable discourse at the opening of this Assembly; and if this be so, what is the duty of the several denominations who have been instrumental indirectly in bringing these great and terrible evils upon our land?

In the halcyon days of the Republic, it was my privilege, for five or six consecutive years, to minister at the altar of this great nation, in the capacity of Chaplain to the Senate of the United States. My position gave me opportunities of information which were enjoyed by comparatively few. Among other things, I learned that statesmen and politicians watched the movements of the Church more closely than we imagined. Nullification was dead and buried; but secession—the disruption of the Union, and the establishment of a glorious confederacy, separate and independent—was among the deceptive dreams of the southern statesmen and politicians even in that day. The division of the Church seemed, in their estimation, to encourage hope and sanction the fearful enterprise.

The great champion of the south, Mr. Calhoun, more than once, in his public speeches on the floor of the Senate, referred with evident satisfaction to the disintegrating policy which the Churches were pursuing; and he appeared especially gratified when those divisions were the result of sectional considerations. The terrible crisis at length arrived—the fatal blow was struck—the Republic trembled from its center to its circumference, and now we find ourselves contending at the point of the bayonet for the integrity of our blessed Union and perpetuity of our institutions.

Whilst, then, the Church, convinced of her error, is endeavoring as far as practicable to repair the damage she has done, let politicians and statesmen imitate her example. Let them come and contemplate this present scene, and catch the spirit of this holy season, until their hearts shall become blended into one great heart of love, affection, and brotherhood. Ignoring politics and party, let them meet on the great platform of a pure and elevated patriotism, and devote all their energies to the restoration of an honorable peace to our bleeding, afflicted, and weary country. And let us, my brethren, cease not, day nor night, to cry unto the Lord God of Hosts, that he would interpose for our speedy deliverance from all the calamities which now afflict us, and bestow a spirit of Christian unity not only upon the Churches, but upon all the people of this land. Then shall we not only see the "stars and the stripes," that glorious emblem of our national renown, waving unmolested in the North, the South, the East, the West, but we shall behold that brighter symbol of our hope and safety, the cross of Jesus, elevated in our midst, and glittering with augmented splendors. Then shall the red battle-field, now vocal with the groans and sighs of the wounded and the dying, become a glorious cathedral, which shall resound only with hallelujahs and thanksgiving to God. Then shall the now sorrowing people of our land unite with descending angels in repeating the heaven-composed song which celebrated the advent of the great Peacemaker between God and man, saying "Glory to God in the highest; on earth peace, good-will to man."

"How long, dear Saviour, O how long
Shall that bright hour delay?
Fly swiftly round, ye wheels of time,
And bring the welcome day."

Mr. John M. Harper spoke as follows:

Mr. Moderator, I regret exceedingly that Judge Sharswood is not able to be present this afternoon, to offer to this body the congratulations of the laity on this occasion, when we have presented to us the prospect of increased usefulness, not only of the portions of the Church which you represent and we represent, but the whole family of Presbyterian Churches. I regret Judge Sharswood's absence the more, from the fact that his acquaintance with Church polity and Presbyterian polemics eminently qualifies him to represent the laity on such an occasion as this, and to express their feelings; I will only say that we shall go back to our people and encourage them, in view of the bright future of which this occasion is the harbinger.

The letter of Judge Sharswood, addressed to the Assembly, was read, as follows:

JUDGE SHARSWOOD'S LETTER TO THE MODERATOR.

PHILADELPHIA, *May* 26, 1863.

REV. AND DEAR SIR: I am informed that I have been appointed by the General Assembly at Peoria one of their delegates to the body over which you preside. It would afford me great pleasure to be present when the delegates are heard; but my official engagements will prevent me; and if present, the fatigue and exhaustion of mind and body consequent upon a long session of the court would incapacitate me from participating. It is, however, of no importance, as my colleagues will fully represent the views and feelings of our constituents on so happy an occasion. I hope, however, to be present at your session some time before your final adjournment. Presenting my cordial salutations to yourself and the members of the Assembly,

I remain, very truly, yours,

GEO. SHARSWOOD.

Rev. Henry B. Smith, D. D., (of New York city,) Moderator, replied in the following eloquent terms:

It becomes my duty, as the Moderator of this Assembly, to make a response to those courteous, those cordial words which have come to us from the kindred Assembly now in session at Peoria. We esteem it a happy circumstance that these words should be uttered to us, that these feelings should be expressed to us, by the reverend gentleman who was the occasion of bringing the subject, in the form in which it finally passed, before that Assembly last year. It is a peculiar satisfaction for us to hear his voice uttering these words, which speak joy and strength to all our hearts; for division, after all, is weakness, and union is strength.

The first time that I ever came to this city of Philadelphia—the first time that I ever attended a meeting of the General Assembly of the Presbyterian Church was in the year 1837—the year to which reference has already been made—the year in which that grand, noble, powerful Church was shaken to its center—the next year to be riven asunder. It was a time when men's hearts were full of anxiety and fear; for, no one could tell what the rupture of such a body might portend either in Church or State.

Since that time we have been separate, but still two powerful growing denominations; for not even division and separation can prevent the victorious progress of our faith and polity in the land. Yet we were sundered from one another, with no words of welcome from the ecclesiastical assemblages to the other—no words of cheer or comfort dropped except as individuals, ministers to ministers, and above all, laymen to laymen. But this separation has been superficial. Deeper than the separation has been and must be the oneness and the unity. The separation belongs to those earthly vestments which see corruption; the unity belongs to that spiritual inheritance which abideth forevermore. Though many years, and first of all among the deepest feelings of the church's heart, this desire for reunion—for the united expression of opinion and feelings, has been growing stronger; and now in the crisis and juncture of our nation's history and threatened separation, these churches are drawing nearer and nearer together; and it may be that our national troubles shall be sanctified to the Church of Christ itself, and unite all that love Christ's name by stronger ties, by undying affinity.

Presbyterians of whatever branch are separated after all, simply by parenthesis and accident of a necessarily temporary nature. Those that have the same standard of faith—those that have the same history—those that have the same polity—those that have the same ends in view, are really one; the differences are nominal and temporary. Our churches, more than we have believed, have been one during all these rolling years; which have witnessed so many bitter words, which now we all repent of and ask God to forgive.

Consider for a moment in what respect we are one. Both these branches of the Presbyterian Church have the same history. Since the first churches were planted here from that noble dispersion which came to us from Scotland and from Ireland, and from England and from the Palatinate to gather themselves under the Presbyterian "order," until one hundred and fifty years since in this city of Philadelphia, they were formed into the first Presbytery, and then one hundred and forty-two years ago were formed into the first synod, and then immediately after our National Constitution was established here, in the same city of Philadelphia, honored ever for its loyalty and its patriotism, and also honored for its devotion to Presbyterianism, were formed into a General Assembly—both the branches of our Church have a common heritage in that long history, that noble descent. We equally own and reverence the names of McKenney, of Andrews, of Finley, of Witherspoon, of Blair, names known and honored throughout the land. We have also the same standards of faith. That matchless Confession, inspired by the deepest genius of the Reformation, formed in the halls of Westminister, and those catechisms, the ripest product of the whole doctrinal movement of the Reformation, in which are gathered together as nowhere else so clearly and distinctly, the most decided teachings of God's word—those belong to us equally. A system excluding Pelagianism, Socinianism and Arminianism—a system Augustinian, Pauline, Reformed and Calvinistic—it equally belongs to us. We confess it in the same words—we teach it in the same formulas.

We also have the same polity—the most honored and the strongest polity that sprang from the loins of the Reformation, with the greatest aggressive organizing power—equally removed on the one hand from prelacy, and on the other hand from independency—that polity belongs to us, one and the same.

We also have the same devotion to this, our beloved country. We are equally devoted to her cause—heart, soul, body, life—ready to give all and do all, that our country may be successfully carried through its conflicts—that this rebellion be overcome, and that we be a united people. Loyalty is the depth of the heart of both our assemblies. We also share in sympathies and prayers for that ill-fated, down-trodden race, placed by Providence in the midst of us, whose burdens lie so heavy upon our nation's heart, and whose oppression lies so deep among our nation's sins. For that race, it is our common prayer that God may open a way for deliverance and elevation, to secure both their good and ours, and to secure the final unity of this our grand, imperial, American Republic.

We are also one in our general aims and spirit as a denomination—as we go forth throughout the land, having for our great object to evangelize this country, and all that come within our borders—to bring them under the spirit and power of the Gospel of our Lord and Saviour Jesus Christ.

Besides unity in all these things, and many more that might be mentioned we also have only one hope, one Saviour, one eternity, one Heaven. We know that whatever the divisions in time, there is to be at last but one General Assembly and Church of the first-born, the names of whose members are written in Heaven.

With the deepest feelings, with the most heartfelt cordiality, we reciprocate all your expressions of kindness and of love, and pray that the Spirit of peace, the dove of heaven, may descend and dwell in the midst of us, and inspire all our hearts. We ask not anxiously concerning the future. We accept what you have offered in the spirit and terms in which it has been communicated. We seek not to cast the horoscope of the future. God alone knows what that may be. It was surely a grand vision that the different branches of the Presbyterian family spread throughout our

Republic, should and could be gathered into one glorious united advancing host, going on conquering and to conquer. But who believes that the wisdom or power of man is adequate to lead or guide such a host? We each have a providential mission, and in that mission our whole object in respect to each other will be to provoke one another unto love and good works, and where the Master has placed us there to labor, relying upon His wise guidance and grace in the future, as we have experienced the same in the past.

Brethren, what a grand and boundless opportunity spreads before these Churches in the future history of our country! If so be that God carry us safely through this conflict and bring us out again into a large and wealthy place, what a work then has God's church to accomplish here upon earth, demanding all its resources, all its energies, all its united zeal, in order that the evils which threaten the safety of our Republic may be destroyed, and that the kingdom of Christ may advance through all our borders—may make the waste places to rejoice and blossom like the rose—may diffuse a pure and undefiled religion, and may bring the gospel of our Lord and Saviour Jesus Christ to bear upon all the institutions, relations and races of men in the midst of us, and thus become our strength, our joy, our peace as a nation enabling us to triumph under the banner of Immanuel, Prince of Peace.

The Church which you represent, we wish God-speed in every good word and work. We pray that they may experience the increase of God. We pray that the blessing of God the Father, and Christ the Son, and the Holy Spirit may rest upon you, upon them, upon us, upon all the Israel of God forevermore. Amen.

The Assembly then united—upon motion of the Rev. T. H. Skinner, D.D., LL.D., in singing the hymn beginning with the words,

"Blessed be the tie that binds,
Our hearts in Christian love."

At the close of this Hymn, during the singing of which the deepest emotion pervaded the Assembly, the Rev. S. H. Cox, D.D., LL.D., at the request of the Moderator, led the Assembly in prayer and thanksgiving in terms eminently appropriate to the occasion, and as we be believe, acceptable to the great Head of the Church.

At the close of these solemnities it was manifest that the members of the body were measurably disqualified for the tedious routine of ordinary business which remained to be transacted, and a motion for adjournment prevailed. This timely interval afforded the members a pleasant opportunity to interchange Christian and friendly salutations, and to congratulate each other *on the appearance of the Bow of Promise in the clouds.* The scene which followed was the most joyous and happy that your delegate has ever witnessed or expects to witness, until the toils and sorrows of earth shall have been exchanged for the peace and bliss of Heaven. The glowing picture of the home of the Prodigal's Father on the return of his lost and wayward boy, as portrayed by the inimitable pencil of *the Divine artist*, furnishes the best scriptural illustration which can now be recalled, with the exception, that there was not present, on this sublime occasion, any visible embodiment of evil passion to represent the Elder Brother, who by his darkened brow might cast even a transient shadow on this bright and cheerful scene. If the same blessed spirit which was illustrated by these proceedings shall pervade, as we know it will, in augmented measure, the General Assembly which holds its perpetual sessions in our "Father's House" above, your delegate feels quite sure that albeit, human infirmity may require the existence of *two Assemblies on earth*, there will be needed but *one Assembly in Heaven!* Even now it would seem that inasmuch as there is but "*one Master*" whom all profess to love and reverence, so there should be but "*one school!*"

Your delegate attended most of the sessions of the Assembly, and united with its members and other Christian friends in commemorating the dying love of the Redeemer. It gives him pleasure to state that he was treated with uniform respect and consideration, oftentimes accompanied with expressions of gratification at the manner in which he had executed his delightful but delicate trust. In justice to himself he may be permitted to say that he is too well acquainted with his own deficiencies, moral and intellectual, to suppose, even for a moment, that these extraordinary manifestations of high regard were to be interpreted as evidences of extraordinary personal worth, but rather as cheerful and merited homage to your venerable Body, and a kindly recognition of the sacred mission which had been inaugurated, in some humble measure, through the agency of your representative.

As the sessions of the Assembly were drawing to a close, your delegate was kindly permitted to obey the impulses of his heart, by giving utterance to the following parting address, to which has been subsequently added a sentence or two, and a verbal alteration:

Mr. Moderator and Brethren of the Assembly: I desire, in a few brief words, before your final adjournment, to express my unfeigned gratitude for the fraternal recognition extended to me as the clerical representative of the Assembly now in session in Peoria. I am grateful for the spiritual banquet in which I was permitted to participate on the occasion of that recognition. I hope, sir,

"While life, or thought, or being last,"

never to lose the impressions of that precious occasion. My soul, sir, has been feasting ever since on the honeycomb which we found in the carcase of the lion we have slain. I am grateful, sir, for the affectionate salutations which I have received personally from scores of the friends of Jesus, the tones of whose voices I had never heard before. I am grateful, especially grateful, for the privilege of uniting with this Assembly, and other Christian friends, in celebrating the holy rite of the commemorative supper. Amidst the highest and purest joys which we can experience on this hither side of the grave, let us never for a moment forget our obligations to Jesus, the perennial fountain of all our enjoyments!

And now that we expect to separate in a few hours, never to meet again in this vale of tears, permit me to express my earnest good wishes for the present and future welfare of the officers and members of this Assembly. My prayer is already up before the throne, that God will take each of you by the hand and conduct you safely along the checquered journey of life, which none can walk successfully alone; and that when you shall have done with the duties and obligations of the present scene, you may all be permitted to join in the deliberations of the General Assembly and Church of the first born, whose names are written in heaven; in that bright and glorious world where change comes not; where separations are never known; where we shall never be called upon under any circumstances, to take the parting hand, or to pronounce the tender, affecting, and sometimes painful word, Farewell!

In returning to our several homes, let us carry with us much of the spirit of the Master, and resolve upon renewed and more entire consecration to his service.

And while the two invincible columns of the sacramental host here represented, panoplied anew with the weapons of light and love, march forward side by side, under the guidance of the great Captain of their salvation, against the common enemy, let them fling out their banners to the breezes of heaven, and inscribe upon their ample folds in golden capitals the felicitous motto indicative of our present ecclesiastical attitude, and beautifully suggestive of the glorious future, when the great ocean of heavenly love shall not be disturbed by a ripple of strife, much less a wave—

"Distinct as the billows,
But one as the sea."

Beloved Brethren in the discipleship and ministry of Jesus, Farewell!

These remarks were responded to by the Rev. P. H. Fowler, D. D., Moderator, *pro tem.*, in the following terms:

DEAR BROTHER: The circumstances in which the overture from your body was accepted by this Assembly, the manifestation of feeling made at the time, and the words of greeting extended to you by the occupant of this chair, assure you of the cordiality with which the proposition for correspondence with your body was accepted by this. Allow me to say that that cordiality has been increased by the truly admirable manner in which you have discharged the delightful and yet delicate part assigned to you.

In parting with you, we beg you to bear with you the assurance of our most earnest wishes for your prosperity personally. We pray that with increasing years you may bear increasing fruits. Be good enough to tender to the body which you represent our assurance of sympathy with them in spirit, and readiness cordially to co-operate with them in the common objects that we propose as Churches of the Lord Jesus Christ. One with them in substance of doctrine, corresponding to them in organization, agreeing with

them in our plans of usefulness, we feel ourselves to be one with them as brethren and servants of the Lord Jesus Christ; and the prayer of all our hearts is, may grace, mercy, and peace be multiplied unto you and unto the dear brethren and Churches which you represent, now and evermore.

Thus ended one of the most delightful missions ever intrusted to mortal man. Your delegate is unspeakably grateful, not only for the distinguished honor which has been conferred upon him by the appointment, but for the measure of success which, by the help of God, has crowned his humble labors.

"*Not unto us, not unto us, but unto Thy name be all the praise, O Lord!*"

In the estimation of many wise and pious persons in both branches of the Presbyterian Church, Providence seems to be shutting us up to ecclesiastical reunion; and if we will only consent to accept and follow His unerring guidance, all will be well. And when these two grand divisions of the Christian Church fall into each other's exceptionless embraces after a constrained separation of a full quarter of a century, there will be experienced an indescribable ecstacy, for which the wide earth can furnish no parallel, and the nuptials will be second in their joyousness only to the bliss of uniting with the Church triumphant, and sitting down with its countless kingly myriads at the marriage supper of the Lamb. If any judge differently of the signs of the times, we would respectfully but earnestly suggest *moderation* in the expression of their dissent so that no new fires may be kindled up, which may, peradventure, require another quarter of a century to extinguish. The calm and conclusive logic of Gamaliel, (see Acts, 5 Chap., 38–39 verses,) is just as pertinent now as when it fell from the lips of the great Jewish counselor, and may be safely trusted in unfolding to us the will of God in this matter. "If this counsel or this work be of men, it will come to

naught, but if it be of God, ye cannot overthrow it; lest haply ye be found to fight even against God."

It is also suggested with equal earnestness and affection, that while we carefully avoid the *Scylla* of *indiscreet opposition* to this great movement on the one hand, we should be equally careful to escape the *Carybdis* of *inconsiderate precipitancy* on the other. Hasty and immature action, though favorable in its aim and intention, may be as disastrous in its results as inconsiderate hostility. A very important advantage has already been secured by the initiatory steps which have been taken by both the Assemblies concerned, and the manifest favor which the measure has received from scores and thousands of our people throughout the land. By what has been done, *we have wiped away the reproach* which, until now, has attached to both branches of the Church in consequence of the hostile attitude which they have maintained towards each other, and which "the great cloud of witnesses" which has surrounded them on every side, has found it difficult, if not impossible, to reconcile with "that charity which suffereth long and is kind." In what we propose hereafter to do in the furtherance of this sublime movement, let us bow down an attentive ear to the sacred oracles, while they announce to us the great lessons of wisdom, by which to control and regulate our action. "Let your moderation be known unto all men. The Lord is at hand." Phil., 4 Chap., 5 verse.

In closing this report your delegate, with the indulgence of the Assembly, will venture a suggestion in relation to a subject which, though distinct, is closely allied to the one which now engages your attention. Some years ago this Assembly was in friendly correspondence with the orthodox churches of New England. For reasons which were deemed sufficient at the time this interchange of Christian courtesies was suspended, and the avenues of intercourse have remained closed up to this hour. As the acknowledged causes of the interruption of the annual greetings are now, in the order of Providence, rapidly passing away, like the shadows of the night before the orient beams, why may not our friendly relations be resumed? Would not the General Assembly add additional lustre to its already bright and glorious record by initiating at the present session such measures as may speedily secure that desirable object? The numerical strength, combined with the religious and intellectual wealth of the Churches represented in this body, accompanied by evidences of the Divine presence, as indicated in their prosperity and advancement, would fully vindicate your motives and place you beyond the range of the most reckless suspicion. Let, then, the great Presbyterian Church, which has covered itself with immortal renown upon a thousand well contested fields of theological warfare in support of the cause of truth and righteousness, be ambitious to exhibit among her bright trophies *the Olive Branch of Peace*, and thus with her unyielding loyalty to Messiah's Crown secure for herself the promised benediction of her victorious and glorified Leader and Head,

"*Blessed are the Peace Makers.*"

To this course of general action we are invited by all the harmonies of nature and the ministries of grace. The providences of God are vocal with expressions of sympathy and kindness as manifested in the success which, through His blessing, has crowned the national arms upon field and flood. The heavy rod by which we have been smitten is already beginning to bud and to bloom, and will ere long bring forth the peaceable fruits of righteousness. Our weary and afflicted country, purified and strengthened by the fearful struggle in which she has been engaged, will soon exchange the armour of war for the insignia of peace. The Stars and the Stripes, the bright symbol of our national glory, tattered and torn by the storm of battle, will wave unvexed in the sunlight of approving Heaven from the Atlantic to the Pacific and from the Saint Lawrence to the Rio del Norte. Hoary *Time*, with his balmy influences, accompanied with the Divine blessing, will, after a while, heal the wounds which have been inflicted upon our proud nationality, and our vindicated integrity be recognized, at home and abroad, to the joy of the wise and the good. Our nation will assume her appointed mission and go forth in the presence of an astonished if not admiring world to illustrate the capacity of man for self-government, and to scatter, *ubique terrarum*, the blessings of religion and civilization. Let us anticipate these developments of Divine Providence and prepare, not only to join in *the full chorus* of a nation's gratitude for the blessing of returning peace to our land, but by our pacific action let us give *the keynote* to the song which shall leap from heart to heart, and from lip to lip, until the blue vault of Heaven shall resound with the rich strains of a nation's joy—ALLELULIA! ALLELULIA!

All which is respectfully submitted.

SEPTIMUS TUSTIN,
Clerical Delegate, &c.

WASHINGTON CITY, D. C., *May*, 1864.

www.ingramcontent.com/pod-product-compliance
Lightning Source LLC
LaVergne TN
LVHW020634110826
845149LV00004B/1183
9781418191603